The Art of the Pendulum

The
Art
of the
Pendulum

Maxi Cohen

Andrews McMeel
Publishing

Kansas City

The Art of the Pendulum

ISBN: 0-7407-3319-2

Contents

Acknowledgments

I want to acknowledge Céu do Mar, a spiritual haven in the heart of Rio de Janiero, the place where in my internal stew this enterprise of writing down the words for *The Art of the Pendulum* came to me. And it is here where I began to see differently and for the first time photograph the beauty of Divine creation.

I want to thank

Scott Flora, Leeloo Thatcher, and Devika Gamkhar, for their help.

Audrey Simmons. In her Venice, California, store, "Audrey's Good Vibrations," when I first showed her these images as artworks, she said she wanted a set and so would others.

Robert Welsch, for his encouragement, wonderful ideas, and great head.

Laura Yorke, for her enduring support and brilliant editing, and for leading me to Carol Mann.

My friends, family, and strangers who along the way picked up the pendulum and began to play, affirming the value of *The Art of the Pendulum*.

• • •

Are you ever stuck? Not sure what's in your best interest? Which choice to make? Many times we do not know what to do; we can't evaluate someone's qualities; we can't discern the cause or remedy for illness. We may not know what job to take, whether to buy or sell, retreat or pursue. Yet deep in our subconscious we have access to a plethora of information about ourselves and others, and the world around us. Gaining access to this knowledge is available to everyone, not just psychics and healers, seers and prophets.

The question is how to access it. That is where *The Art of the Pendulum* is most useful. The pendulum is a tool used to access one's truth, or one's absolute inner knowing.

What Is a Pendulum?

A pendulum is a weight suspended on a string. The weight can be made of brass, copper, glass, wood, almost anything; but the shape is best when the bottom is pointed. The string can be silk, cotton, metal, gold; any material will do. A pendulum can be store-bought or homemade.

 History of the Pendulum

The pendulum has been used for hundreds of years by professionals and laypeople to find hidden treasures, diagnose disease, and locate missing persons, even gems beneath the earth. Predating the pendulum, dowsing or divining rods were employed to discover where water, oil, or minerals existed underground. The words *divining* or *dowsing* are often associated with the pendulum, even though the pendulum's range of use is far more extensive.

There is evidence that the Hebrews, Egyptians, Persians, Etruscans, Druids, Greeks, Romans, Hindus, Chinese, Peruvians, and Native Americans among other cultures used divining rods in some fashion. The first record of divining is thought to be an eight-thousand-year-old cave painting at Tassili n'Ajjer in the foothills of the Atlas Mountains in the Sahara. The scene is a crowd of tribesmen intently observing a dowser searching for water.

Divining rods were already used in Egypt a thousand years before the Dead

Sea parted and the Hebrews fled for the Promised Land. The Bible speaks about Moses using his staff for the purpose of finding water: "Thou shalt smite the rock, and there shall come water out of it, that the people may drink" (Exodus 17:6). "Take the rod . . . and speak ye unto the rock . . . and it shall give forth . . . water" (Numbers 20:8). When the Queen of Sheba came to Jerusalem in the eighth century B.C. to seek the wisdom of King Solomon, she brought with her diviners who sought water and gold along the way. Before King Solomon consorted with the exotic queen, he used a diviner to confirm

. . .

his union. According to Plutarch's *Life of Marcus Antonius,* Queen Cleopatra, reigning in Egypt fifty years before the birth of Christ, traveled with at least two dowsers who were always in search of gold.

From China, India, and Africa come references to using rods for finding lost objects as well as subterranean treasures. Throughout Europe there is mention of the use of rods in folklore and in the writings of monks from the twelfth to the fifteenth centuries. Yet during the Middle Ages through the Inquisition, there were incidents of imprisonment as the rods were considered "black magic." In A.D.

1528, Martin Luther denounced divining as being the work of the devil; he cited dowsers for breaking the First Commandment regarding idolatry. *De re Metallica*, a book by Georgius Agricola (1556), described and illustrated the use of divining rods in mining metallic ores. A carving on the handle of a miner's tool used in Saxony between 1664 and 1749 shows the scene of a diviner in search of ore. By the seventeenth century, divining in the mining industry was common in England as well as throughout Europe.

In the seventeenth century, Kaspar Schott, a Jesuit priest and mathematician, theorized that the movement of the dowsing rod was due to unconscious muscular action. In 1799, Professor Gerboin at the University of Strasbourg brought a pendulum back from India and presented it to the Academy of Sciences in Paris, after which he wrote a book about his experiments with metals.

Abbé Mermet, a French priest and pioneer in the field during the early 1900s, successfully dowsed for water and minerals in Africa by first holding a pendulum over maps at his home in a French village. After solving inquiries from around the globe, including locating missing persons

• • •

and helping the Vatican solve age-old archaeological problems, Mermet was honored by the French National Society for the Encouragement of Public Welfare. Concurrently, Frenchman André Bovis, a professional food taster, used the pendulum to test the quality of cheese and wines. He constructed a special pendulum, made of crystal with a fixed metal point at the end that hung from a string of red and violet silk. Using his pendulum, he could rate the vibratory radiations of food.

In the early part of the last century, after World War I, there was a movement toward scientific research using the pendulum in many applications, particularly in the field of medicine. Dr. Albert Abrams published a book in the 1920s about the use of the pendulum in detecting and treating disease. In his work, he discovered how the body broadcasts high-frequency radiation from cells, indicating disease or health. He even discovered how the body itself could be used as a pendulum by using one's center of gravity as the pivot point.

It has been reported that during World War II, the pendulum was used by British Intelligence to determine Hitler's next attack! During the Cold War, "Verne"

Cameron, an American dowser, was able to locate the position of submarines and bases in the Pacific, and could even distinguish which were American and which were Russian. During the Vietnam War, Marines used pendulums to locate underground mines, tunnels, and booby traps.

Even corporations have used the pendulum! Contrary to those who pigeonhole the pendulum as a new age, subjective, juju device, it is interesting to note that Bristol-Meyers, Hoffmann-LaRoche, and RCA have paid dowsers to locate resources.

When it comes to science, Albert Einstein and Nobel Prize winners in Physiology and Medicine, Dr. Alexis Carrel (1912) and Charles Richet (1913), were fascinated by how and why the pendulum worked in terms of the physics of motion in relation to various forms radiating energy. Additionally, one of the first properly conducted, double-blind studies with statistically valid results was carried out by two skeptical engineers (Chadwick and Jensen) at the University of Utah in 1971. The results of their careful research concerning magnetic fields and dowsing showed dramatic evidence affirming the power of dowsing. More scientific studies have followed yielding similar results.

. . .

Nevertheless, in the end, a pendulum cannot be used without a person, and it is the subconscious of the person that influences the direction in which the pendulum moves.

Today, the pendulum is used by medical practitioners, including doctors, medical intuitives, chiropractors, and nutritionists for making diagnoses as well as determining treatment. Depending on the movement of the pendulum as it is held over different parts of the body, a doctor can determine the location of infections. By placing the pendulum over remedies, the ones most beneficial for the

· · ·

patient will stimulate the pendulum to move in that direction and away from remedies that would not be useful. Furthermore, the pendulum can be used to determine accurate medicinal dosages. Some practitioners teach their clients to use a pendulum so they can check, each day, which supplements and medications their ever-changing bodies need.

Divining has been used to locate lost articles or people, the source of physical or mental ailments, ley lines and their direction of flow and effect on human health, power centers and places where the Earth's field alters human consciousness, as well as radiation and energy fields. In addition, it has been used to analyze chakras and auras. The pendulum is becoming ever more popular as a tool for discerning how to respond to the most intimate dilemmas and worldly issues.

Why Use a Pendulum?

As the pace of life gets faster, we often need to make decisions at breakneck speed. We don't always have the time for quiet reflection and rumination to discover what is bubbling below the surface. And even when we do, we don't always find the answers. The pendulum can provide access to what we know deep inside. It can be used by itself or with the cards in this kit.

Using the Pendulum

Anyone can use a pendulum. The more you practice, the more adept you will become. The more your mind and your ego stay out of the way, the more successful and accurate the results will be.

What to ask

The pendulum will respond to any question that requires an either/or, yes/no, or multiple-choice answer. Your questions have to be phrased in a clear and specific manner. Your nervous system cannot translate an essay question to the pendulum for an answer. Ask what concerns you now.

What not to ask

Don't use the pendulum to read the future, such as asking "will I marry George?" The answers you get are based on the circumstances now. You can ask, "Is it in my best interest to marry George?" Don't ask two questions at the same time, such as, "Is it better for me to move to London or Paris?" It is a good idea not to ask frivolous questions or those you already know the answers to, except in the beginning, when finding answers to easy questions will help build confidence. Don't ask the same question over and over again; you probably just didn't like the original answer and are trying to sway the pendulum in the opposite direction. Don't ask questions when you are weak, tired, or unfocused. Being firm, aligned, and awake will work to your advantage.

Holding the Pendulum

Hold the chain of the pendulum loosely between your thumb and forefinger or middle finger. Allow as much of the string as you need for the pendulum to move freely, let's say two to four inches. Keep relaxed; don't be tense. Make sure you are grounded, comfortable, and not tired. A good position would be sitting upright in a chair, feet uncrossed on the floor, and the elbow of your arm holding the pendulum on the table. Relax. Don't be distracted by other people, the television, or anything else in your environment. It's important to be totally present and completely focused on what you are doing.

Pick a card that will answer your dilemma
Concentrate on what you wish to ask, aligning your body, mind, and spirit. Each of the twelve cards will be explained below, so you can choose the best one to answer your need. *Make yourself tranquil.* This is most important and may be the hardest for you, but to get an accurate reading *your mind and emotions must be in a neutral state.* It is easy to influence the pendulum with your subjective desire. One trick you

might use is to repeat to yourself, "I wonder what the answer will be?" over and over, leaving no room for desire to sneak in. You must have nothing invested in the answer, as if you were reading the weather report in China.

Place the pendulum at the center point of your choices

This is often at the bottom of the card, but on some cards it may be in the center.

State your question
as specifically as possible

You can do it out loud, if you wish, or silently to yourself. Then relax, be patient, and ask, "I wonder what the answer will be?" Once you have an answer, you can always use your pendulum to recheck, by asking, "Is this true?"

A good way to begin is to use the Divining Wisdom card. Place it on the table before you. Hold the pendulum over the center bottom; ask, "Which direction is YES?" After the pendulum makes its way in that direction, ask, "Which direction is NO?" These simple questions will help affirm your confidence in using the pendulum. The more you use the pendulum, the easier it gets.

Getting Started
with
the Cards

The Art of the Pendulum cards can be consulted on any matter, problem, or decision you need to make regarding business and personal issues. They can help in understanding the nature of other people, your spouse, lover, friend, boss, and employee, prospective or current. Whether it is when,

• • •

what, or how, the cards will help you with whatever you need to know.

You can use the cards with the pendulum or as art for contemplation and beauty. For example, if a card reflects a question in your life, place it over your desk for a week. Set an objective so that the answer will make itself known. You can do this simply by declaring your intention to yourself. You might not be certain whether to take a safari to witness the birth of elephants next month, or to stay and take on a special project that's been offered to you. Place the Divining Journey card on your desk. Say to your-

· · ·
24

self, "By the end of next week, I intend that the answer will be crystal clear to me. I am not going to think about it or obsess about it anymore. By then, I will just know." Through the power of your word and your intention, the answer will come. The card will act as a placeholder for all your concerns.

If the beauty of an image or the poetry of the words resonate with you, place the cards in special locations—on your altar, your vanity mirror, in your foyer, next to your bed. Let the cards be a source of contemplation.

• • •

• • • DIVINING WISDOM • • •

This is a good card to start with to become familiar with the way the pendulum works. At first ask it easy questions like, "Do I live in the United States?" or "Am I a woman?" It is encouraging and exciting to see the pendulum go in the direction of a truth you know.

Now try it with an unresolved problem. Maybe you need to make a decision; you feel paralyzed and can't act. You might need to know: "Should I accept that job?" "Is this used car a good invest-

• • •

ment?" "Is my mother right?" Condense your dilemma to a YES or NO question and ask what you need to know now.

••• DIVINING LOVE •••

Almost everyone at one time or another wants to know what their love life holds. You're involved with someone and you're not sure what it means. What is it you're really feeling? What does your heart and body know that you are not sure of . . . yet? How do you feel about your old boyfriend? Or about the woman who pursues you now?

If the pendulum doesn't move, you

might want to go back to the Divining Wisdom card and ask, "Is it worth spending more time with this person?" "Is it in my best interest to maintain a platonic relationship?" "Is it a good idea to open my heart more?" For every question you have, there will be a card that will show you the answer.

••• DIVINING TIMING •••

Timing is everything. Being at the right place at the right time, or speaking out at the right moment can be critical. Some people consult astrologers and numerologists for advice on when to take action. You

•••
28

can use the cards to help you in a flash, anytime, anywhere. When is it best to start a new venture? When should you go on vacation? Purchase that stock? Propose marriage? Follow up on a job interview? Consult the cards to be in the flow. One way to double-check your answer is to see how your body responds. Often a feeling of "right" will resonate or confirm your intuition. Use this card whenever you are uncertain if you should act now or later.

··· DIVINING JOURNEY ···
Notice how every move you make determines the next step on your journey in

life. Sometimes it's hard to choose what to do. Your mind tells you one thing, your heart another, or a small inner voice suggests something that makes no sense. Under those circumstances, doing the irrational thing can be scary. Sometimes you have no criteria on which to make a decision; other times you can see things from so many perspectives that nothing feels quite right. Get quiet and use this card to guide you: What's your next move? Should you stay at your job or seek another? Is it best to stay close to home, or take a trip? Should you leave the relationship or stay? Do you go on a

. . .
30

spiritual journey, or stay and progress with your profession? If the next question after receiving the response GO is WHEN, use the Divining Timing card.

··· DIVINING LOCATION ···

Do you feel like you're living in the wrong place? Some locations make life easy, rewards come, and other settings feel like dead ends. Often we don't even know this until we are forced to consider change. Where to move is a big consideration. This card can help take the anxiety out of the issue. It's useful to approach the cards like a game, as if nothing is invested in the answer. It is a way to take the dilemma from inside you to outside you for a breath of fresh air. What if, who cares, let's see. Figure HERE is where you are, and THERE is any place you choose it to be. Where should you live? Work? Raise your family? Deliver the truth? Meet your destiny? Where is the perfect place?

••• DIVINING AUTHENTICITY •••

When you don't know what the truth is, or what you are feeling, seeing, or hearing, this card can help. If you don't trust your perception about another's integrity, using the pendulum over this image of the crop circle will inform your perception. Is your partner being real with you? Are you being real with yourself? It is in the precise asking of the question that the truth can be revealed.

••• DIVINING ABUNDANCE •••
When we have money, time, joy, and knowledge, we have a choice in how to handle our resources. For example, you have an opportunity to help a fledgling company. Do you barter your services for stock? Invest your own money? Save your money and time and use it elsewhere? Spend your resources without

any compensation? What about your inheritance? Do you invest it in tech stocks? Save it for the future? Spend it on a vacation? Barter it for art? Rather than fret over your abundance, use the pendulum to seek what's in your best interest.

··· DIVINING WELLNESS ···

Something feels like it may be wrong, or you just may want to check to be sure. There may be an issue with your teeth, your hormones, your stress level, even your diet. This card will help you to know what is going on inside your body. Ask a question about your concerns and learn if you are fine, or if you need to check it out, or simply just wait and see. If CHECK IT OUT is where the pendulum points, think about the various ways to do this. Use the Divining Choice card to know what to do or pay attention to first.

••• DIVINING CHOICE •••

Sometimes you are faced with too many choices. Where to go to school? Which doctor to see? Where to take a vacation? Which investment to make? Turn your dilemma into a multiple-choice question by assigning each potential answer a letter on the card. Let the pendulum tell you

•••

which choice is in your best interest. (It may help to write down what each letter stands for, so you don't forget. For example, where should I go on vacation? a) Carnival in Rio; b) archaeological site in the Gobi Desert; c) Italian monastery. Once the choice is obvious, go for it!

··· DIVINING VALUE ···

This card will help you to evaluate the value of things and people in your life. Imagine that 100 is dream perfect and 0 is empty and of no benefit. Find out how valuable a vacation, a person, a remedy, a book, or even using the pendulum will be for you.

···

For example, you might want to know how much value you would get if you went on a spiritual pilgrimage to Medjugorje. It is important to be specific. So you may need to ask, how much value would you receive if you went there with your sister? Then ask, how much value would you get if you waited and went at Christmas with your parents? Or you may wish to ask the worth of pursuing each of your projects at this time? Or you may want to know, if you went out with so-and-so again, how worthwhile would it be? Rate your experience.

* * *

··· DIVINING CREATIVITY ···

There is a time for gestation and a time
for leaping into the void. Sometimes we
are not connected enough to the cosmos
or to our inner selves to know which is
the correct action to take. When we dive
and the timing is wrong, we might just
hit muck. When our heart cries for diving
and we hesitate, we miss the opportune
moment. Use this card to know if it's time
to stop pushing your creative juices and
just receive in retreat, or whether to go
for a breakthrough.

Ask if now is the time to dive deep by
putting the house up for a second mortgage

···
38

to finance your first feature film, or to play it safe and seduce investors. Ask if you should invite the woman you just met on a two-week rafting trip with you, or make a date for when you return. Ask if going hang gliding, taking up ceramics, or a long nap is the right move. Ask if it is time for stillness or time for hurtling yourself into the unknown. Then trust the response you get.

• • • DIVINING GUIDANCE • • •

You hear a voice inside you, an intuition, a stirring . . . perhaps in a dream, a conversation, or in line at the supermarket. Is this the voice of Divine wisdom, your highest potential, your purest heart, or is it the voice of your ego (inflated or not)? To be conscious and understand why we do things makes our lives meaningful. In moments of uncertainty when we cannot discern the guidance, or the impulse to do something, asking the question, "Who's speaking?" might help you choose.

For example, you want to save the world by creating a show that promotes nonviolence, even though you have no experience. You're a dentist. Is this a Divine mission you should pursue, or is it just the voice of grandiosity? Something

· · ·

keeps telling you to quit your job. Is this laziness, fear of success, or your self-destructive ego at work? Or is it perhaps the Divine Creator calling you to a higher purpose? You find yourself obsessing about moving your family to the country. Is this fear (ego) or the Omnipotent Protector leading you to safety? If the pendulum swings toward God, trust, have faith, and go for it!

Using the pendulum alone

You can also learn to use the pendulum without the cards. One way to test which way is YES for you and which is NO is to ask, "What does YES look like?" The pendulum will most probably move to the left or right, or clockwise or counterclockwise. It's a good idea to respect this extraordinary power. Saying thanks when it responds is a way for you to appreciate the value of this gift. (Some people are so awed that the pendulum actually moves on its own accord, that they respond cynically. Creating opposition will not help you.) Then ask, "What does NO looks like?" Most often, the NO will be the opposite movement from YES.

It is important to be patient and quiet. Do not get easily discouraged if the

• • •

pendulum does not move right away. Concentrate your thoughts on the pendulum, not the movement you anticipate it making. The key is to stay relaxed and attentive.

You can test your ability by discovering what foods might be best for your body right now. For example, take a glass of milk or an orange and put the pendulum over the object and ask, "Is this good for me to have at this time?" Then try it with juice; next coffee. You may wish to start with something you are sure is good for you, and proceed to something you're not certain about.

Advance this process by testing a group of things to determine which may be best for you. Pour a small amount of milk in one glass, tap water in another, wine in a third, mineral water in a fourth. Ask, "Which is best for me?" and see where the pendulum goes.

Accuracy

Once you have an answer you may wish to test it against another system, the I Ching, the Runes, and so on. Nothing is infallible. You may discover that if you act against the wisdom you receive, the results will not be to your liking. It happens. Using the pendulum should be approached with seriousness, but not obsession. Be grateful and humble that you can access the truth in such mysterious ways.

Why the Pendulum Works

If you're very sensitive, you know that you can have a feeling or even a sensation in your body in response to a person who is dangerous or creepy and a very different response to one who is loving or possesses healing energy. Not everyone is this in touch. When the pendulum moves it is amplifying the signals that our nerves wish to communicate to us. It makes the subtle obvious. This is one of many scientific theories about why the pendulum works, yet no one knows for sure.

The pendulum alone does not give you the answer. It does not make one up, separate from you. It reveals what you already know to be true deep inside yourself. Some people know what is right (or not right) for them by what they feel in their bodies. For example, you might have a gut reaction, an actual tangible feeling in your gut that you don't like or trust someone. Or a voice on the phone might make you tense or make your heart open. For those who cannot perceive these subtleties, what the pendulum does is demonstrate what our inner higher intelligence is communicating through the nervous system, delineating the YES/NO codes set by the conscious and subconscious minds.

If you have a dog, you may notice how she reacts to people. Many guard dogs can sense if a person is friend or foe without even seeing the individual. They bark at some who pass outside the house and not at others. Some dogs will run to greet their masters at the gate before they arrive. The pendulum is a way for our psyche to be made evident to our conscious selves by magnifying these subtle frequencies.

There are astrological explanations, spiritual hypotheses, dowser theories of "radiation" or perceiving "wavelengths," the science of radiesthesia, and probably more rationalizations for why the pendulum works. Yet no one theory is for certain. Once you see that the pendulum works for you, you won't care why it does. When asked, "What's electricity?" Thomas Edison replied, "I don't know what it is, but it's there, let's use it."

. . .

A Tool Forever

The more you use the pendulum, the more comfortable and relaxed you will be with it and the quicker it will give you an answer. With time, the many ways it can serve to help you will become evident. Carry the pendulum in your pocket or purse. Take the cards with you on vacations and business trips. You will find that you will not seek advice from others as often. You will no longer need to tolerate responses that do not apply to you. With the pendulum, you are asking your most intimate higher self for answers. You are asking the Divine Source in you, your own wisdom. The responses you receive are what you would tell yourself if you had perfect hearing and the inner silence to know everything always. So use the pendulum wisely, but also have fun with it.

About the Author/Artist

Maxi Cohen is an artist, author, and independent film, video, and television director/producer. Her films play on television and in movie theaters. Her artworks are in the permanent collections of the Museum of Modern Art and the Metropolitan Museum of Art in New York City, the Museum of Fine Arts in Houston, and the Israeli Museum in Tel Aviv.

Photograph Index

. . .

7. **DIVINING ABUNDANCE:** Sedona, Arizona
8. **DIVINING WELLNESS:** Desert Botanical Garden, Phoenix, Arizona
9. **DIVINING CHOICE:** Ben Lomond, California
10. **DIVINING VALUE:** Los Angeles, California
11. **DIVINING CREATIVITY:** Botanical Gardens, Rio de Janeiro
12. **DIVINING GUIDANCE:** Palm Springs, California

. . .

Bibliography

Hansen, George. "The Trickster and the
   Paranormal." *Journal of the Society for Psychi-
   cal Research.* 51:792. (October 1982):343–67
http://www.tricksterbook.com/
   ArticlesOnline/Dowsing.htm

Nielsen, Greg, and Joseph Polansky. *Pendulum
   Power: A Mystery You Can See, a Power You
   Can Feel.* Rochester, Vermont: Destiny
   Books 1977.

http://www-sop.inria.fr/agos-sophia/sis/
   dowsing/dowsdean.html

• • •

http://www.wlake.com/hicks/dowse2.html

http://mypage.direct.ca/j/jliving/
    landmine.htm

http://www.accessnewage.com/articles/
    mystic/DOWSING1.HTM